WATERSIDE WALKS
AROUND
NORTHAMPTONSHIRE

by
Tony Noble

JEMA PUBLICATIONS

Published 1992 by Jema Publications

Copyright 1992, Tony Noble

ISBN: 1-871468-03-5

Publishers' Note

Every care has been taken in the preparation of this book. The publishers cannot accept responsibility for any inaccuracies or for any loss, damage or inconvenience resulting from the use of this book.

Illustrations by Elizabeth Noble

Published by:

Jema Publications

40 Ashley Lane

Moulton

Northampton

NN3 1TJ

CONTENTS

NORTHAMPTONSHIRE

- location of the walks

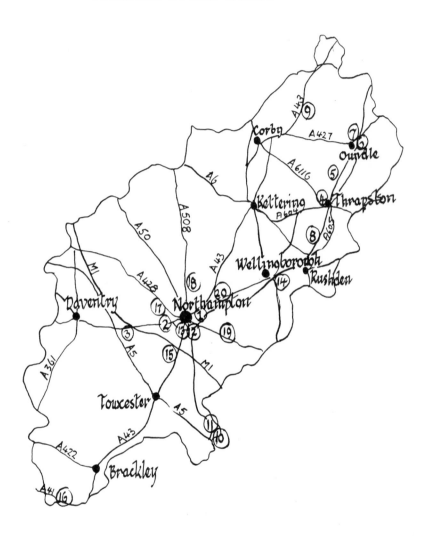

INTRODUCTION

Welcome to this collection of twenty waterside walks around Northamptonshire. It has been written with **families in mind**. Many walks often become a "hard slog" covering far too many miles. These are all meant to be enjoyed and of a reasonable length - the longest is under 7 miles and all are without steep gradients and heavy walking. Each walk is circular to avoid any retracing of steps.

The walks cover some of the most beautiful countryside that you will find in Northamptonshire. Within each walk there will be places to stop, explore and picnic but also keep your eyes open and you will see a variety of water birds and animals. Explore the mills on the River Nene, the nature reserve around Titchmarsh or find out where and what is the Iron Trunk.

How long?

Each walk highlights interests and attractions for all ages and is intended to take up the best part of a half or whole day. Allow yourself extra time to explore and enjoy your surroundings - it is better to have time on your hands and explore further, than to have to rush to complete the walk. A rough guide is to allow a pace of one mile an hour for young children, increasing this to about two miles an hour for ten/eleven year olds.

What do you need?

Always be prepared for the worst weather. The British climate can change very quickly. Walking boots or strong shoes are preferable to flimsy plimsoles or wellingtons. It is also better to wear several thin layers of clothes and peel off as it becomes warmer - one thick jumper gives limited options! Waterproof kagoules or something light and similar are essential. Try to avoid jeans - in wet weather they cling to the legs and become uncomfortable, cords are better. Finally, do not forget your camera, simple spotter guides, binoculars, picnic food, maps and perhaps a towel..... but do not be overloaded, that is just as bad as not having the essentials. A small rucksack will be useful.

With children slight accidents may happen - it would be wise to take a few first aid plasters!

Remember water can be dangerous. Stay away from the edge of the water and walk on the paths. Do not wade in the water, the depth can be deceptive. Do not pollute the rivers or canals. Watch small children at all times.

Routes

The maps in the book, together with the directions supplied, should prove adequate for following your route. As far as possible all routes have public rights of way but occasionally these are altered. The detour will hopefully be shown, but where a right of way crosses a field, that for instance is now supporting crops, be sure to respect this and walk around the edge.

For those who wish to carry an Ordnance Survey map the following 1:50000 Landranger series cover the relevant walks:

Walks 4-9, 18 ...Sheet 141

Walk 6 ...Sheet 142

Walks 1-3, 10-15, 17-20 ...Sheet 152

Walk 16 ...Sheet 151

Every effort has been made to ensure that descriptions of the walks and the accompanying maps are accurate, but this cannot be guaranteed. Things change - footpaths become diverted and overgrown, towpaths eroded, footbridges blown away, and signs and landmarks disappear. I hope that you will not encounter such problems, but if you do, the publisher will be pleased to have details.

Enjoy the walks.

Respect the countryside.

Observe the Country Code.

Good walking!

SYMBOLS USED ON THE MAPS

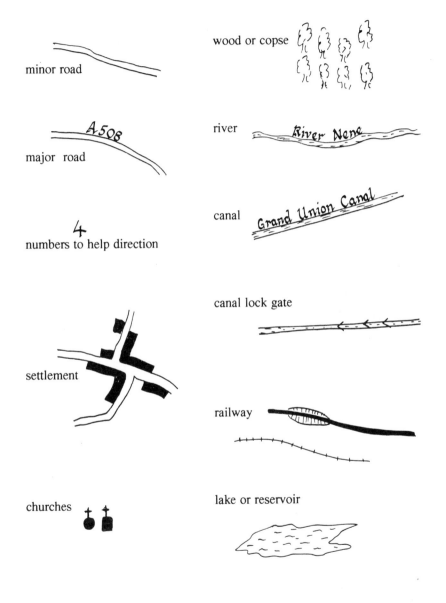

minor road

major road

numbers to help direction

settlement

churches

wood or copse

river

canal

canal lock gate

railway

lake or reservoir

ACKNOWLEDGEMENTS

My sincere thanks go to my daughter, Elizabeth who has produced all the drawings and been very patient with my demands. My thanks also to my wife and son who have joined me on several of the walks and offered useful constuctive comments.

WALK 1   4 miles

Weston Favell Mill - River Nene - Billing Aquadrome - Clifford Mill - Little Houghton - Weston Favell Mill

SUMMARY: A short and easy picturesque walk along the backwaters of the River Nene with the opportunity to see an abundance of birdlife and one of Northamptonshire's prettiest villages. Binoculars will be useful. A view of the motte of Clifford Hill is very impressive. Families can enjoy a mid-walk break to Billing Aquadrome and Mill with the chance for refreshments and for the children to relax on the play equipment. There are many informal picnic areas throughout the walk.

ATTRACTIONS: There has been a mill at Billing since before the Norman Conquest, but the present one was built at the beginning of the nineteenth century and restored in 1967. Situated within the grounds of Billing Aquadrome the working machinery is clearly seen as the water quickly turns the giant wheel. It is fascinating to stand and watch the water being thrown over the wheel blades, and to imagine the human activity generated by this. Other machinery, millstones, tools and photographs give a nostalgic look at our past.

Centuries ago there were certainly mills at Weston Favell and Clifford but today all that remains are a series of lock gates. Close to the river and a little way into the walk you will have the opportunity to see Clifford Hill - a large circular mound and ditch. Called a castle motte, although there is no evidence that there ever was a castle built upon it, this is one of the largest mottes in the country. Constucted soon after the Norman Conquest it is strategically placed at the crossing point of the river and near to the mill and was a defence against an incursion by the enemy.

It was along here that John Clare (1793-1864), perhaps the county's most famous poet, often wandered from his imprisonment in a lunatic assylum. He even wrote of his experiences.

With the help of the Lord's of the Manor, Little Houghton has developed its character over the centuries and many of the buildings

1

were built between 1600 and 1750. The church, originally of the twelfth century, was built by William de Houghton and much was rebuilt during the nineteenth century. The village stocks can be seen near the village Post Office.

Throughout the walk there is the opportunity to spot the wide variety of water birds, wild plants, flowers and insects.

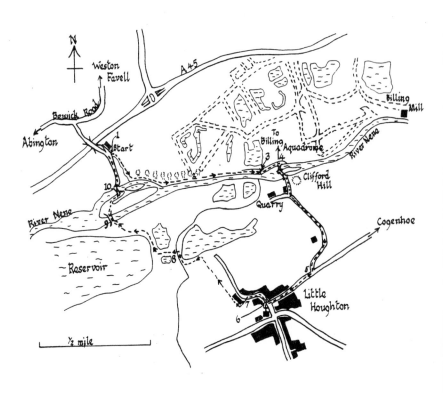

START: Weston Favell Mill lies 2 miles east of Northampton and about three quarters of a mile from Weston Favell Church. Park the car in the cul-de-sac lane off Bewick Road and crossing over the A45 Wellingborough to Northampton new dual carriageway. The lane leads to the mill and Northampton Boat Club.

ROUTE: A signpost into a field indicates the footpath to Great Billing Mill. Do not follow the lane through the gate to the Boat House.

Cross the stile (1) into the field and walk alongside the stream. The path curves around to meet the River Nene at the picturesque moorings of Northampton Boat Club. This route is also part of the long distance Nene Way footpath and signs to this affect appear.

Continue alongside the River Nene walking adjacent to a beautiful line of poplar trees. After a short while a stile (2) marking the boundary of Billing Aquadrome is reached. Consideration for dogs here as built into the stile is a dog hatch! On the right hand side of the river is a lake - look for the bullrushes, coots, moorhens, swans and grebes.

Continue over the stile and along the banks of the River Nene. Keep to the right of the stream, following the footpath signs. Cross the bridge over the weir (3) and the land opens out by Clifford Hill and locks.

At this point (4) and before continuing the walk enjoy a visit (in season - April to October) to Billing Aquadrome and Mill.

Continue the walk by turning over the bridge and walking towards Clifford Mill House. Pass the house on the right and walk through the gate and along the left trackway looking back at the impressive views of Clifford Hill Motte. On the right is Clifford Hill Quarry.

The road curves around to the right and after about three hundred and fifty yards meets the minor road between Cogenhoe and Little Houghton (5). Turn right and walk along the footpath into the village.

This leads into Station Road. Turn right into Meadow Lane (6) and down the hill. On the corner is 'Sundial House'. Look for the sundial above the top window of the house. Also note the steps which could have been a milk churn stand or a horse mounting stand!

A few yards down the hill and at the second sharp turn, look for the public footpath sign to Great Houghton (7). It is on the left and points towards a private house and driveway. The path is on the left of the drive.

Cross over the stile and into the field. Turn immediately right and walk alongside the garden fences and through the gate into another field.

The path through the field follows a line of small trees and leads to a gate on the far side. Ahead are gravel pits and many different birds. Cross over the stile by the gate and turn left along the track. After a few yards the footpath turns right, continuing alongside the gravel pits.

In a few more yards turn left over the stream and stile (8). Walk straight ahead between the two lakes. Turn right alongside the larger of the lakes. The path curves around to the left and in the distance you will see the Northampton Boat Club House.

The track opens out to reveal a reservoir on the left and brings you to an iron bridge over the river (9). Cross the bridge. Go over the stile to the right and make for Weston Favell guillotine lock gate (10).

Turn right along the path and then left returning to the lane and your starting point.

WALK 2   3 miles

Kislingbury - Upton Mill - Upton - Kislingbury

SUMMARY: An easy walk along the River Nene's plain with the chance to observe and admire waterbirds and wildlife.

ATTRACTIONS: Kislingbury dates back to Anglo Saxon times but it is the associations with Cromwell and the Civil War for which it is remembered. The New Model Army, under General Fairfax of the Parliamentarians, established head quarters in Kislingbury, several days before the Battle of Naseby. Cromwell's troops joined the army at Kislingbury.

Upton village is now deserted and all that remains are irregular humps and mounds around the area. The Hall, dating from the seventeenth century is now a private school. The grounds are said to be haunted by the White Lady of Upton who visits at midnight when there is moonlight.

Upton Mill is in a beautiful setting and used to be one of the many working mills along the Nene. The mill is first mentioned in the Domesday Book of 1086 and belonging to King William I was let for 12s 8d a year. Throughout the centuries it has had several owners and in 1815 was completely rebuilt prior to cease grinding corn in 1900.

Upton Mill

5

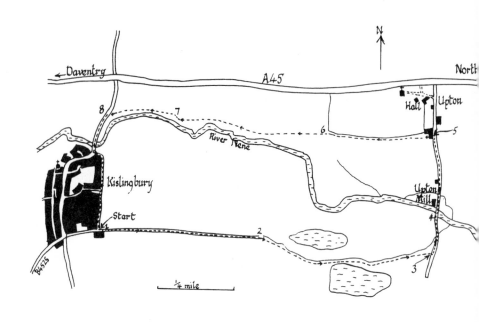

START: Kislingbury village is situated four miles west of Northampton and on the A45 road to Daventry.

ROUTE: Begin your walk along the back lane farm track (1), passing Hall Farm immediately on your right. This lane is hardly ever used and on either side is a mass of wild flowers - rosebay willow herb, campion, blackberries and nettles. The Express Lift Tower, a landmark in Northampton is clearly visible on the skyline.

Continue along the lane and through the gate at the end (2). The farm track continues beside a stream with forget-me-nots, wild rose and thistles in abundance.

The footpath, although not well marked, continues between two lakes. Grebes, swans and coots enjoy the peace and tranquility, whilst dragonflies dance around the edge of the lakes. A beautiful setting and so close to Northampton!

Follow the stream around to the left and Upton Mill appears ahead. Look for the farm gate (3) on the right. Through the gate and continue left along the track and over a wooden bridge towards Upton Mill. The mill, surrounded by pasture land, is now privately owned, but with the traditional mill pond is a photographer's paradise.

Pass through the gate and alongside the mill (4). Continue down the road, through farm buildings adjacent to the lane. Beyond these buildings is a house on the left. Look for the Nene Way footpath sign on either side of the lane (5). Turn left by the old milk churn stand and walk through the farm yard.

The route is clearly marked over a stile and along the perimeter wall to the grounds of Upton Hall.

At the end of the first field there is an interesting old footbridge, no longer used, but once forming part of the Nene Way.

Continue to follow the line of the old wall which leads into the next field. A beautiful old metal ladder-stile, with a hand rail is almost lost in the undergrowth adjacent to the next gate (6). It marked the route of the Nene Way.

Cross the centre of the next field, overgrown with thistles, poppies and clover. Kislingbury Church appears on the horizon.

Make for the stile in the left hand corner. Continue into another overgrown field which has been left to waste. Walk alongside the hedge which is immediately on your left. About three quarters of the way around the field there is a gap in the hedge (7). The footpath turns left through this gap and continues across towards the right hand corner of the field.

Go over two stiles, both marked with the Nene Way sign. The second stile points diagonally across the field towards the road.

Turn left (8) along the road and over the narrow bridge and return to the village.

The Common Dandelion

WALK 3   5 miles

Flore - Nether Heyford - Heyford Mill - Flore

SUMMARY: A pleasant walk along the valley of the River Nene, which also follows a picturesque area of the Grand Union Canal. The two villages, like many in Northamptonshire have character, charm and historical interest.

ATTRACTIONS: Although the origin of the village name is unknown the name Flore has, over the centuries, been associated with Flora, and possibly named after the beautiful Celtic maiden who also had connections with Julius Caesar. Since 1890 traditional May Day festivities have been celebrated. The village school children have elected a May Queen each year since 1890.

Nether Heyford is famous for its five acre village green and the Manor House. The Manor House and parkland, the latter being sold for development in 1975, is said to have once been owned by Francis Morgan, Judge of the King's Bench, whom it is thought pronounced the death sentence on Lady Jane Grey.

Heyford Mill although recorded in the Domesday Book lies derelict and idle, but was once an important mill on an important transport route.

Both village churches date back to the thirteenth century. Flore has medieval doors and doorways whilst Nether Heyford has many memorials and carvings to admire.

Watling Street, which the walk crosses on two occasions, was once a Roman road originally stretching from Dover to Chester. It derived its name from a group of Saxon settlers, the 'Waedingas', who lived near Verulanium (St Albans).

Bluebell

9

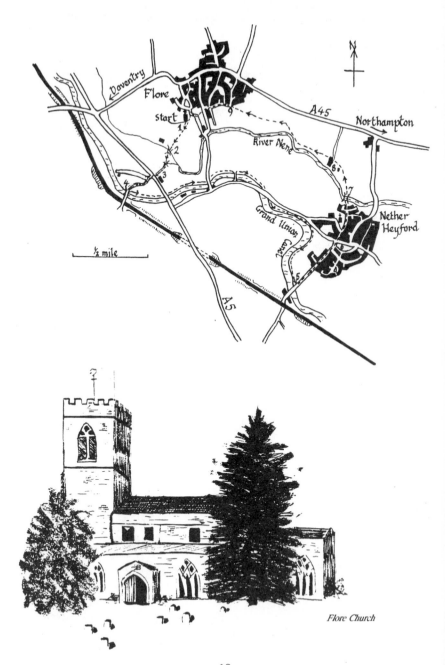

Flore Church

START: Flore is situated on the main A45 Northampton to Daventry road and close to junction 16 on the M1 motorway. Park in the village of Flore and begin your walk by All Saints Church.

ROUTE: Take the footpath through the churchyard and leading to a gate marked Nene Way (1). Walk across the field, diagonally to the right making for a farm building and footbridge (2). Cross the footbridge and over the River Nene and following the Nene Way signs. Turn immediately left, walking across the corner of a field to another footbridge over a tributary of the river. Turn right after crossing the second footbridge and walk alongside the stream towards the house and garage on the main A5 road (3).

Cross over the A5, but be careful, and follow a footpath sign and the Nene Way along a farm track. The track curves around to the left with Flore Cemetery across a field to the right. Turn right just before the bridge (4) and down to the Grand Union Canal towpath. Immediately on the towpath turn left under the bridge. Do not follow the Nene Way footpath.

Follow the towpath passing back under the A5 and alongside some of the most beautiful canal countryside in the county. After about two miles leave the towpath and take the footpath onto the red and black brick bridge (5), which forms part of Furnace Lane leading into Nether Heyford. Also advertised on this bridge is the Foresters Arms.

Continue left along the lane into Nether Heyford. The Baptist Church is on the right by the village green (6). This is a good place to stop and rest. The village green covering five acres is one of the largest in the country! Refreshments are available at the shops or the Foresters Arms.

Continue the walk by crossing the road at the junction of the Weedon Road and the Bugbrooke Road and by the War Memorial. Walk down Church Street to the right of the memorial. The street meets a dead end by the Manor House. Follow the footpath sign past the Manor House and out into a small housing estate. Turn left and look for the marked footpath by the lamp post and between houses 34 and 36.

The path leads to a footbridge (7) over the River Nene. Walk over the bridge and continue straight ahead along a wide well worn track. Continue over several stiles - marked the Nene Way, past an old ox hovel and rejoin the Nene Way footpath. The old Heyford Mill (8) and pond stand in a lovely spot, derelict and forlorn. With the mill on the left continue over a footbridge and stiles, across the farm lane and over another stile into a field.

The walk continues to follow the well marked Nene Way footpath.

Keep close to the field fence on the right. Cross over the stile in the corner of the field and again keep close to the fence. The hedge soon turns right leaving fifty yards of open field. Keep straight ahead making for two stiles and a footbridge.

The walk continues across open pasture land, passing under electricty pylons and over a stile making for the right hand corner of the field. Cross over a stile and turn sharp left keeping the hedge on your left, but soon bear right to find a stile between two hedges.

Climb over the stile and walk diagonally right towards the houses and the footpath sign. Through the gate (9) and back into Flore village. Continue down King's Lane and into Nether Lane. Turn right into Spring Lane and then almost immediately left past the playing fields and along the path to the school and church.

Nether Heyford War Memorial

WALK 4 4 miles

Islip - Islip Mill - Titchmarsh Nature Reserve - Aldwincle - Islip

SUMMARY: A gentle walk along the valley of the River Nene with the opportunity to view a variety of bird and butterfly life in Titchmarsh Nature Reserve. Binoculars will enhance the enjoyment of your walk.
ATTRACTIONS: Islip Church has connections with George Washington, first President of the United States of America. Mary Curtis of Islip married Sir John Washington who was great, great, great uncle of the President. A monument to Mary Washington is found on the south wall of the chancel. The village of Thrapston, separated form Islip by a medieval nine arch bridge also has Washington memorials in the church of St James'.

Islip Mill, in an idyllic backwater of the River Nene, is now a private residence but until 1960 it was still used to grind corn.

Titchmarsh Nature Reserve is known for its variety of birdlife - grebe, bittern, sandpiper, goosander, redshank and plover are all found here. A wide variety of butterflies and dragonflies make this area, which was once old sand and gravel workings, a nature lover's paradise.

Yellow Iris found in marsh land.

13

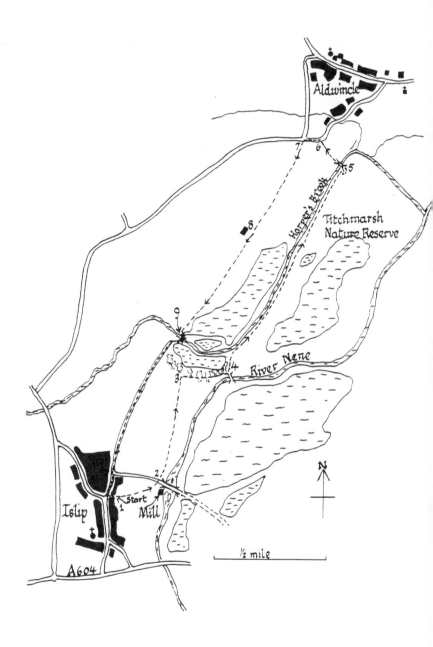

Aldwincle

Titchmarsh
Nature Reserve

Harper's Brook

River Nene

Islip

Mill

Start

A604

N

½ mile

14

START: Islip is situated on the A604 about half a mile from Trapston. There is ample parking in the village. The walk begins at the Rose and Crown public house in the High Street.

ROUTE: The first part of the walk follows the Nene Way footpath. Find the sign at the entrance to the Rose and Crown car park (1). Walk through the car park and garden to a stile.

Climb over the stile and continue diagonally right across the field. Over another stile and again diagonally right across the next field, towards the bottom right hand corner. Two stiles either side of the lane take you into a field (2).

It is worth a detour down the lane to see the old Islip Mill.

The footpath, marked the Nene Way, leads through the middle of the field, to meet a gate on the far side. I walked for a few minutes along the banks of the River Nene and was lucky enough to see dragonflies and damselflies.

The Nene Way is marked at the gate and in the middle of the next field. Make for the two stiles leading into the wood. Turn right (3). The path is well marked along the edge of the wood and leads to the lakes which were once sand and gravel workings. This area really is a beautiful part of the Northamptonshire countryside. There are many picnic areas between here and Aldwinkle.

Continue along the path until reaching the footbridge. Turn left over a stile (4) and into Titchmarsh Nature Reserve. Walk alongside the lake and turn right at Harper's Brook. The nature reserve is alive with wildlife and is an ornithologists paradise - grebes, common tern, redshank, greenshank and common sandpiper to name but a few.

Follow Harper's Brook through the nature reserve and over several stiles until reaching the sign for Titchmarsh Nature Reserve on the far side. Go left over a stile (5) marked the Nene Way and across a footbridge over the river.

The path continues along a farm track and through a field until meeting the village lane. Do not turn right into Aldwinkle, unless visiting the village, but left along the lane (6).

At the junction turn left (7) down a farm track marked 'Elinor Trout and

15

Fishery'. At the end of the track and by the farm buildings (8) go over a stile and into a field adjacent with Titchmarsh Lakes. Walk through the field keeping close to the right hand fence.

As you reach the end of the lake, and about thirty yards before the corner of the field, bear left to the footbridge (9). This takes you around the back of the lake.

Go over the footbridge and into a farm track beside a lake and woods. The walk continues through a gate marked footpath and bridleway.

The gravel track lane takes you back to Islip. Look to the left and you will notice the River Nene and the earlier part of the walk.

Aldwincle - **Wadenhoe** - Achurch -

Thorpe Waterville - Aldwincle

SUMMARY: A walk along the Nene valley with superb views between Aldwincle and Wadenhoe. The villages are full of historical intrigue and charm. There are many picnic areas and several public houses offering refreshments.

ATTRACTIONS: Wadenhoe Church built about 1250, like many small churches, has charm and character. It is situated on an isolated knoll and the Norman tower has a saddleback roof. An interesting memorial is on the north wall. A sad tale of how Thomas Welch and Caroline his new wife, daughter of the rector of Polebrook, were shot by Banditti in Italy whilst on honeymoon on 3 December 1824.

Aldwincle was the birthplace of John Dryden, who became the Poet Laureate in 1670. He was born in 1631 and spent his childhood in Titchmarsh, but the Dryden family home was Castle Ashby. There is a memorial to Dryden in All Saints Church, now no longer used and opposite the church is the Old Rectory, now named Dryden House. Dryden developed the ability to appease who ever he was writing for and to manipulate words for different occasions. His first published work was a glowing tribute and celebration to Cromwell. Next year he switched allegiances and welcomed Charles I in his writings! As the Poet Laureate he was paid £300 a year, but in 1688 he fell out of favour and was relieved of his position. When he died he was buried in Westminster Abbey.

Aldwincle has the distinction of having two churches. In the Old Rectory of St Peter's, now sadly pulled down, was born Thomas Fuller in 1608, another famous literary figure. He eventually became Chaplain to Charles I.

The River Nene at Wadenhoe broadens out and divides into two with one of its channels rushing over the ford beside the old mill. This ford gives access to the island formed by the river. There has been a mill on

17

this site since Saxon times, the current one falling into disuse in the nineteenth century, was renovated and is now a private residence.

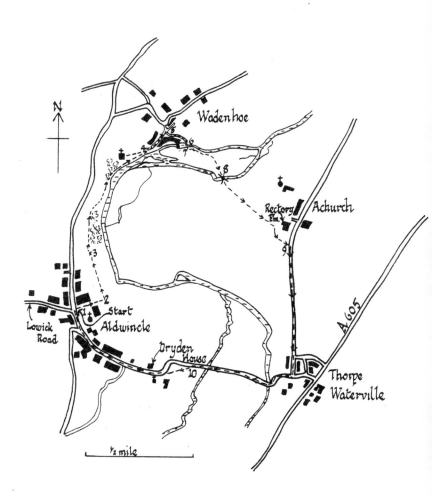

START: Aldwincle is situated about 2 miles north of Thrapston and just off the A605 road to Oundle. There is ample parking in the village. The walk begins by St Peter's Church. Aldwincle has two churches, be careful to get the correct one.

ROUTE: Opposite the turn down Lowick Road find the stile marked the Nene Way (1). Cross over the stile into a small field with buildings to the left and the church to your right.

Two more stiles come in quick succession, the latter leading into the edge of the field. There is also another footpath coming from the right.

Turn left (2) which is the route of the Nene Way. Begin by keeping to the edge of the field. Soon the path continues through the centre of the field before meeting the hedge on the left.

Look for the delapidated stile (3). Over the stile and into the adjacent field. The hedge is now on your right. Becareful at this point not to continue with the hedge on your left. Here the walk offers superb views of the Nene valley.

Continue alongside a wood. Cross over two stiles either side of a small footbridge. The path curves through a field of pasture keeping within a few yards of woodland area.

The walk opens out beside the river with boggy ground to the right. A haven for dragonflies with ragged robin in abundance - a beautiful spot.

Two Nene Way signposts direct you through a wood of mixed trees - lots of wild roses to admire. A stile at the end of the wood directs you left and up a slight incline. In a few yards a sign post sends you back into the wood.

The walk is well marked and opens out into a lovely picnic spot by the River Nene. A gate finally opens out into a field with Wadenhoe Church to the left and the village ahead. It is worth spending a while exploring the church (4).

Continue along to the village. Walk up the road passing The King's Head on the right. The footpath and the Nene Way turn right at the end of the street (5). Continue around to the left and down to the river.

The river opens out to a ford (6) beside the old mill. There has been a water mill here since Saxon times. A sign post to Achurch directs you along a path and over a bridge straddling the River Nene (7). Follow the Nene Way sign beside the river.

After the first field and where the river bends, make for a footbridge directly across the field (8). This area of the walk is an island trapped and surrounded by the River Nene as it meanders through the pictureque countryside.

Cross the footbridge marked the Nene Way. Walk with the fence on your left to the corner of the field. Over a stile. Do not follow the Nene Way straight ahead and towards the church, but follow the hedge to the right up a slight incline and over a stile.

The walk continues between a fence and a hedge before going over a gate. This part of the walk is not well marked. Make for the farm buildings ahead and then detour around to the right. A stile takes you into a lane. Turn right (9).

In about half a mile you reach the village of Thorpe Waterville. At the end of the road turn right towards Aldwincle.

After the third bridge look for the finger post sign to Aldwincle, situated and disguised in the hedge on the left (10). Over the stile. Walk diagonally to the right across the field. Two stiles help you cross a farm track. Meet the road again and turn left towards the redundant church of All Saints.

Continue past Dryden House on the right and return to the village.

Cowslip

WALK 6   4 miles

Oundle - Ashton Mill - River Nene - Oundle

SUMMARY: A pleasant gentle walk starting in the historical market town of Oundle and following the picturesque Nene valley. An alternative route is possible by following the footpath to the right off the bridge. The path then follows the River Nene to point 6.

ATTRACTION: The visitor to Oundle could be forgiven for thinking that it was a university town, so grand are its buildings. It is in education that Oundle has its fame for here is a famous public school, and the houses and ecclesiastical buildings give it a pedagogical atmosphere. There are many fine buildings highlighted in the town trail which is available locally. If you have time, do spend a while exploring the town.

Although the early part of the walk follows the edge of Ashton it is worth taking a detour to look at this charming and peaceful village, which has its claim to fame with the Annual World Conker Championships held every October on the village green.

Ashton Mill now a museum was in regular use during the nineteenth century. Then in 1900 the mill was converted by Lord Rothschild into providing piped water to the village and electricity to the main buildings and farm. Quite a feat for the Victorian era. The museum includes a wonderful collection of farming implements, a variety of fish tanks, a forge with tools and equipment, and craft displays on thatching and basket making.

21

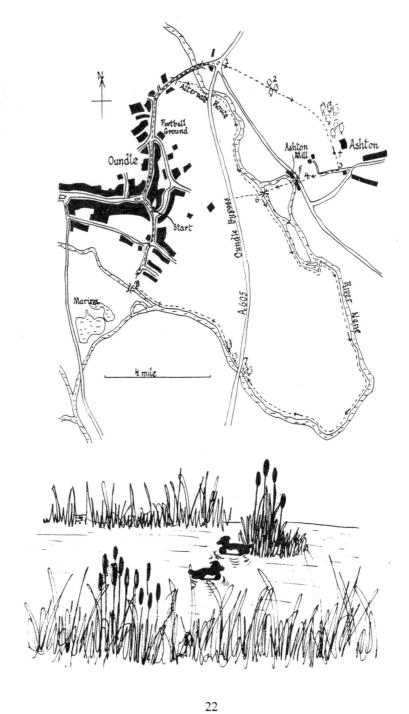

START: Oundle is situated just off the A605 midway between Thrapston and Peterborough and on the A427 to Corby. There is ample parking within the town. I used the car park down St Osyths Road leading off from the Market Square.

ROUTE: From the car park in St Osyths Road walk towards the Market Place and then turn immediately right along North Street, passing many of the houses belonging to Oundle Public School. Continue past the football ground and on towards the famous old bridge built in 1570.

Do not take the footpath leading off the bridge and to the right unless you wish to miss out Ashton. If you take this route along the river then pick up the walk at point 6.

Continue up to the roundabout which takes traffic from Oundle bypass. Look for a stile (1) and the sign post directly opposite on the far side of the roundabout and off the Ashton Road.

Over the stile. Walk straight ahead and along the side of the field with the hedge immediately on your left. Just like 'Watership Down' around here with all the rabbit burrows.

Pass through the group of trees (2) in the left hand corner of the field and out into a further field, again walking alongside the hedge which is on your immediate left. The path is not well marked here. Make for the stile in the far left hand corner of the field. Over the stile, straight ahead and follow the edge of the field and wood which curves around to the right.

Look for Ashton Chapel on your left. Built in 1706 the Chapel, School and Schoolhouse were endowed "for bringing up and instructing the poor of Ashton". Exit the field through the gated cattle grid (3) and turn right into the lane.

If you wish to explore the village turn left.

The walk, which is now part of the Nene Way, continues past the entrance to Wise Weighs House on the right and through a gate sign posted public footpath. Walk directly across the middle of the field (4), the path is partly worn, until meeting the gate the other side. This is the main village road to Polebrook and it is here that the walk is marked the Nene Way.

23

Turn right along the road. After a few yards turn left (5) at the Nene Way sign and through the grounds of Ashton Mill. The mill is worth a visit if you have time. The walk takes you past the idyllic mill pond, through a gate and down towards a footbridge and the River Nene. This marks the junction of four marked footpaths (6). Turn left following the River Nene and the Nene Way.

The next one and a half miles follow the banks of the river through beautiful unspoilt countryside. Look for wildlife. I enjoyed the company of a flock of Canada Geese, an isolated heron and a water vole skuttling along the river bank.

A total of nine stiles take you to the road bridge and the Oundle bypass traversing the river.

Pass under the bridge (7) and through a small wooded area before going over a stile and into an open field. Continue along the river bank following the river as it branches away from Barnwell Marina. Turn right at the footbridge (8) and across the field towards Oundle. A sign post and stile take you into a lane and on towards the town.

Walk up the lane and bear right at the top. Do not turn immediately right into Hern Road but bear left. Continue down towards the car park in St Osyths Lane.

24

WALK 7   3 miles

Cotterstock - Oundle - Cotterstock

SUMMARY: The walk traverses either side of the River Nene between Cotterstock and Oundle and provides for a pleasent half day walk. This can be extended further by visiting Oundle, an ancient market town dominated by the splendid old buildings of Oundle School.

ATTRACTIONS: Cotterstock, a peaceful and quiet village, was frequently visited by John Dryden, the Poet Laureate, and it is here in the Hall that he wrote his Fables. Cotterstock Hall was built in 1658 and the estate was sold in 1927. The mill was built during the nineteenth century and sadly destroyed by fire in 1968. Cotterstock village dates back to the Domesday Book and there was certainly an early settlement by the river as a Roman Villa with mosaic flooring was discovered here.

There is much to see and admire in Oundle. St Peter's Church, the old Talbot Inn built in 1626 and having connections with Fotheringhay Castle, and the old Oundle School built in 1556 with buildings scattered around the town. One of the school buildings is the Latham Hospital in North Street - it was here in 1611 that Latham founded a new school and almshouses.

Cotterstock Mill

25

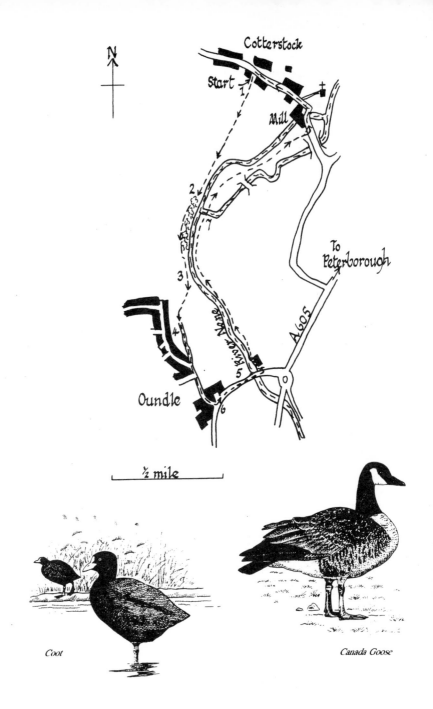

Cotterstock

Start

Mill

To Peterborough

A605

River Nene

Oundle

½ mile

Coot

Canada Goose

START: Cotterstock is situated north of Oundle just off the A605. Park in the village and begin your walk opposite Gatehouse Cottage and Cotterstock Hall. The footpath between two houses is sign posted.

ROUTE: Walk along the path between the houses (1) and up to a marked stile. Climb over the stile and keeping the hedge on your left walk along the well trodden path and down to the corner of the field.

Continue over the footbridge and alongside the wood (2) with glimpses of the river through the trees. The path continues through several fields and over numerous streams until reaching a stile and small water works. Climb over the stile with the water works on your right and then continue straight ahead across the field (3).

Cross over a small fence and stream and onto a well marked path. Oundle church can be seen in the distance.

The next field leads through to the playing fields of Oundle Rugby Club. Continue straight ahead and out into Occupation Road - a minor road with access to tennis and a bowls club (4).

Continue down the road and into St Peters Road.

At the junction of New Road there is a pleasant picnic area by going over the stile to the left, across the field and down towards the bridge and the river (5).

The walk continues down New Road past the playing fields on the right and along to the main road (6). Turn left and over the bridge. On the parapet of the bridge there is an inscription recording the rebuilding of the bridge in 1570 due to its destruction by flooding.

Take the first left marked footpath which leads down to the river and the boathouses.

The walk continues alongside the River Nene, perhaps the only sound is a passing boat or the rustle in the weeds of a moorhen or coot. Enjoy the peace and tranquility as the footpath leads over a weir and towards the guillotine lock (7).

A flock of Canada Geese enjoy the meandering river as it divides to join up again beyond the old mill.

Cross the lock continuing along the river and island to the mill and the country road leading back into Cotterstock.

Turn left along the road and back into the village.

WALK 8   5 miles

Kinewell Lake - Woodford - Denford - Ringstead - Kinewell Lake

SUMMARY: This is a lovely easy walk through beautiful countryside and following closely the River Nene. There is an idyllic picnic spot by the lock just before the disused railway bridge. An additional or shorter walk around Kinewell Lake is worth considering.

ATTRACTIONS: Kinewell Lake is situated on old gravel workings and is a haven for migrating birds and wildfowl.

Woodford Church of St Mary the Virgin, dating back to the Norman era, stands majestically on the banks of the River Nene. Situated in one of the pillars on the north side of the nave is a glass case containing the remains of a human heart. It was probably found during restoration work in 1867 and is possibly that of a knight returning to the village after the Crusades, or even perhaps that of one of the descendants of the lord of the manor. Certainly an interesting feature in the church.

Ringstead, derived from the Anglo Saxon meaning "circular place" is first documented in 1124. The oldest building in the village is the thirteenth century church of St Mary - the architecture is of Early English and the Decorated period.

Denford is a beautiful village and a detour to the walk would be to follow the river along the main road. It does so for almost a mile and then continues into Thrapston. Denford with its Aylesbury ducks has an appealing seductive charm, which captures the imagination of rural Northamptonshire.

Mills were common place along the river and there were two, at both Denford and Woodford. On the early part of the walk you can still see Willy Watt Mill containing two water wheels, one of which can be seen at the right hand end. The mill was used for paper making.

29

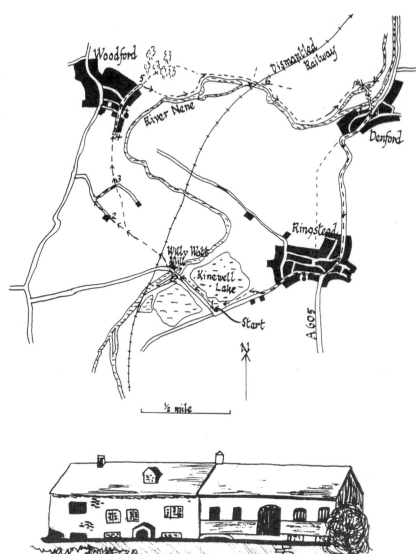

Woodford

River Nene

Dismantled Railway

Denford

Ringstead

Willy Watt Mill

Kinewell Lake

Start

A 605

N

½ mile

Willy Watt Mill

START: At the car park just off the Ringstead to Great Addington road. Use the second car park off the road dividing the two lakes. Ringstead is on the A605 and can be reached off the new A45 bypass.

ROUTE: Leaving the car park (1) walk alongside the lake and parallel to the road making for Willy Watt Mill. At the top of the lake turn left over the stile and onto the road. Continue over the river and past the mill.

Immediately past the mill and on the right is the Nene Way footpath sign. Follow this over two stiles and across several fields towards Woodford. The Nene Way signs are well marked and the path well trodden.

Leave the Nene Way and walk past farm buildings on the left and onto a farm track (2). Go over a cattle grid and turn right down a farm road. Rejoin the Nene Way on the left (3). Climb over the stile walking along the Nene valley, keeping the fence on your left.

Climb over another stile and walk towards the houses and gate. Do not go over the stile to the left but take the stile into the lane with the houses on the right (4). This follows the Nene Way footpath into the lane. Woodford Church appears on the right.

Continue past the church and along Church Street with the old school on the right. The Nene Way follows a different route but our walk rejoins it later. The road ends in a cattle grid (5). Cross over this and into a field. At this point there are two marked footpaths. Take the one bearing right and down towards the river.

The footpath is well marked and soon rejoins the Nene Way by the river. This part of the walk is exceptionally beautiful and peaceful with the footpath clinging to the banks of the river. There are many picnic areas, especially across the lock and on the small island to the right.

At the lock there are two marked footpaths. Follow the one immediately ahead and signposted the Nene Way. This leads through a gate and over the dismantled railway. Through another gate and immediately turn right and down to the river (6).

Turn left along the river bank and make for Denford. Cross two stiles before reaching the bridge. Cross over this bridge and two more into

Meadow Lane. This leads into the main road. The walk continues by turning right at The Cock public house but for a detour through Denford and another riverside walk turn left. This is a beautiful spot and well worth exploring.

The return journey from Denford is just under a mile along the road and into Ringstead. There is a footpath through adjacent fields but it is very badly marked.

When in Ringstead turn right past the church and walk alongside the lake to the car park.

WALK 9   3.2 miles

Blatherwycke Village and surrounding lake

SUMMARY: A walk around Blatherwycke Lake, a haven for bird life and through typical Northamptonshire countryside.

ATTRACTIONS: Blatherwycke is a quiet village with a beautiful medieval bridge having date stones as early as 1656. The Stafford family having married into the O'Briens were prominent within the village and surrounding area and stones inscribed with their intertwined initials are found on the bridge and house opposite. Holy Trinity Church is now closed for services and is in the care of the English Heritage. The church has some fine tombs of the O'Briens who were the Earls of Stafford and who originally owned the Hall, which was pulled down some sixty years ago having been built in 1713.

Blatherwycke Lake is teeming with waterbirds and an ornithologist's paradise. There is a large flock of Canada Geese. It is possible that the lake is the largest man made lake in the county and was dug by Irish labourers and used as a source of water for the iron works at nearby Corby. The demise of the steel industry is the waterfowls gain!

Early into the walk there is rather a strange statue isolated in a field. The Greek Archer well weathered and looking forlorn and dejected is said to be in memorial to a pet!

Returning as you will along the road is Blatherwycke Mill sadly neglected but a most austere and impressive building.

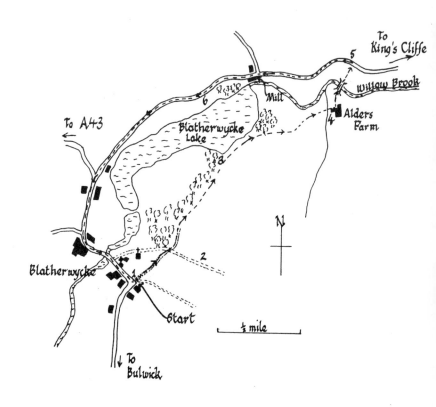

To King's Cliffe

5

willow Brook

To A43

Mill

Blatherwycke Lake

Alders Farm

4

6

3

N

2

Blatherwycke

1

Start

½ mile

To Bulwick

34

START: Blatherwycke is north of Corby on the Bulwick to Kings Cliffe road and situated just off the A43 Corby to Stamford road. Park your car in the area between the bridge and the bend leaving the village to Bulwick.

ROUTE: Walk towards the sharp right hand bend on the Bulwick road. Take the left farm track leading down past the church (1). Look for the statue (2) up on the right and glimpses of the lake on the left.

Continue along the track by the side of the wood. There is a row of horse chestnut trees in the wood and the path disappears where the wood and the lake meet. At this point there is a beautiful view across the lake and a bed of bullrushes (3).

Although the path is not well marked continue alongside the lake and fence, past a small copse, and on towards Alders Farm. Change fields at a suitable point and move down towards Willow Brook. The path continues to be obscure but observe the country code by walking around the field, and head for the farm (4).

Turn left between the farm house and the cottages and walk towards Willow Brook. Cross the bridge and then turn left at the road (5). Continue along the road reaching Blatherwycke Mill on the left in about half a mile.

Soon after the mill the small wood gives way to an open field leading down to the lake (6). Sadly the bird life on the lake must be viewed from the road. Binoculars are essential but spend a while admiring the activity.

The walk continues back along the road, past the Wakerley signpost and down into the village.

The Iron Trunk - Walk 10

WALK 10   4 miles

Cosgrove - The Iron Trunk - Old Wolverton -
Wolverton Mill - Cosgrove

SUMMARY: A walk which begins in Northamptonshire and leads into Buckinghamshire before returning back to your original county. But who minds crossing the border? The countryside is so picturesque, quiet and peaceful and begins along the Grand Union Canal and includes the Ouse Valley Park. This walk is ideally suited for the winter or wet weather as the route is almost entirely on hard man-made paths and where not, there are suitable alternatives.

ATTRACTIONS: There is the opportunity to look at the 'Iron Trunk' built in the early nineteenth century. The magnificent view of the aqueduct with its silver and red colours standing out against the green vegetation of the Ouse Valley is superb. The aqueduct stands 36 feet above the river and is 101 feet long and 15 feet wide and was finally built after several attempts had ended in disaster. The River Ouse marks the boundary between the two counties and is the beginning of the Ouse Valley Park. This is an area of particular beauty with walks and opportunities to see wildlife, flora, fauna, a railway viaduct, a working farm, an old mill and even a little of true history with a motte and bailey mound! What more on a walk than to see herons, moorhens, kingfishers, little grebe, dragonflies and a wide variety of butterflies. Take your binoculars, keep your eyes open and with a little luck you may spot the unusual. Throughout the Ouse Valley Park there are interesting information boards and maps!

The motte and bailey castle mound near to the old medieval village of Wolverton was an early defence system, built to watch the Ouse Valley.

Wolverton Water Mill was built in the late eighteenth century and repaired in 1983. The cheap water energy which turned the wheel was perhaps used to grind the corn.

Cosgrove

Grand Union Canal

River Tove

N

1
Start

8
2

7

3

River Great Ouse

A5

Mill

Alternative Route

4

5

Car Park
6

A5

½ mile

Dragonfly

START: Cosgrove is situated two miles north east of Old Stratford and just off the A508 to Northampton. Your starting point is the Barley Mow public house situated in a road called The Stocks. As you will see from the map there are several car parks around the walk and these can also be used as starting points. Refreshments are available in the Barley Mow or approximately half way round the walk at The Galleon. Both pubs have canal side gardens.

ROUTE: From the Barley Mow (1) walk down the hill towards the tunnel leading under the canal. Walk under the canal - mind your head - and then immediately turn through 180 degrees and back up to the canal side. Turn sharp left along the towpath. You soon arrive at Cosgrove Lock, Cottage and Marina (2). Here "Linda Cruises" offer narrow boat trips and also 'horse and cart' trips to the Barley Mow! Is the beer that strong?!

Look for the milestone indicating that it is 27 miles along the canal to Braunstone. Continue towards the aqueduct with Cosgrove Park on your left. The Park is a hive of activity in the summer with children's play areas and camping facilities. The aqueduct is reached in about five hundred yards (3). Cross this, go down the path to the left and under the canal. Stand back and look - you will be rewarded with a magnificent view of the 'Iron Trunk'.

You are now in Buckinghamshire, but do not let that worry you, the Ouse Valley Park has splendid walks.

Having admired this great feat of engineering, return to the canal side and continue your walk towards Wolverton - a distance of about six hundred yards. Just before the bridge, take the left path to the road (4). Turn right over the bridge and continue along the road. The bumps and hollows in the field to the right are all that remain of the medieval village of Wolverton. Soon a path to the right leads down to the church and to a good view of the motte and bailey castle mound (5). This castle overlooked the Ouse Valley and would have been a dominating feature during the twelfth century.

Continue along the road, bearing right into the old road, now a cul-de-sac. In a few yards again turn right into the more busy main road. Fortunately the walk along here is very brief passing Wolverton Park

House Boarding School on your right and new developments on your left. Look for the picnic sign pointing right and the marked sign, 'Public Footpath To Riverside Walk' (6).

Turn right and walk along the track. A car park is on your left. After about three hundred yards is Wolverton Mill, now a farm and quiet backwater of the River Ouse. Although I did not see one, I am told that the lesser spotted woodpecker frequents this area.

Just before arriving at the mill, there is a choice of return walk of the same distance. You can, if you wish, walk alongside the River Ouse and through the Ouse Valley Park back to the 'Iron Trunk'. From there re-trace your steps to the Barley Mow. This is the better winter route.

For the other route, continue through the gate after crossing the river. Turn diagonally right and make for a delapidated stile. The path is not well marked but cross three fields, then through a gate and towards the wooded area by the canal (7). In the distance you can see Cosgrove Church.

The path alongside the wood now becomes more distinct and eventually leads to the marina and canal lock.
Through the wood you may hear the hum of narrow boats on the canal. As you approach the end of the wood cut through a well marked track to meet the canal side with the marina to your left (8).

Cross over the lock and re-trace your route to the Barley Mow.

WALK 11   5miles

Cosgrove - Grand Union Canal - Furtho - Cosgrove

SUMMARY: A pleasant amble along the Grand Union Canal towards Yardley Gobion and across the main A508 making for Pottersbury. Return to Cosgrove through the attractive Northamptonshire countryside meeting the Grafton Way at Furtho.

ATTRACTIONS: Cosgrove's geographical position, bounded by the Rivers Ouse and Tove, has, over the years, encouraged settlers and there is evidence as far back as the Romans that the area was occupied. The building of the Grand Union Canal in 1805 increased the industrial development and today the canal and Cosgrove Park attracts many visitors.

The oldest building in Cosgrove is the church of St Peter and St Paul with its tower rising above the local houses. The chancel dates from about 1180 and outside on the eastern end are the remains of a typical Anglo-Norman triple window and arcading. Also outside on the north wall, are pillars and an arch of a late thirteenth century doorway. Although the chancel arch was damaged by fire in 1586, it is possible to see a late medieval wall painting on the wall above the arch. The church had extensive restoration during the eighteenth century.

Perhaps one of the most idyllic spots in all these walks, is the area around Furtho. All that remains of this former medieval village is St Bartholomew's Church, situated in a field with a pond close by, and a few yards away, a fifteenth century dovecote. The dovecote, built of local limestone used to hold 330 nests. The village was depopulated during the seventeenth century by Edward Furtho and by early in the next century, only the church, one house and the dovecote survived. The house was later demolished and the present Manor Farm built.

41

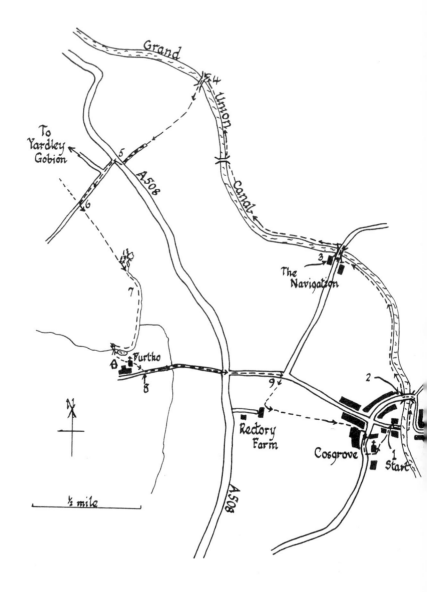

Grand

Union

Canal

To
Yardley
Gobion

A508

The
Navigation

Furtho

Rectory
Farm

Cosgrove

Start

N

½ mile

A508

START: Cosgrove is situated 2 miles north east of Old Stratford and just off the A508 to Northampton. Like Walk 10 your starting point is the Barley Mow public house (1) situated in a road called The Stocks. This and the other Cosgrove walk can be added together to make a longer one if required. Refreshments are available at the Barley Mow where there is also a canal side garden.

ROUTE: From the Barley Mow walk down the hill towards the tunnel leading under the canal. Walk under the canal - mind your head - and then immediately turn through 180 degrees and back up to the canal side. Turn sharp right along the towpath. Immediately across the canal and to your left are large gardens descending to the canal side, one of these belongs to the Barley Mow.

You soon arrive at a picturesque and highly decorated Gothic stone bridge (2). Obviously the remains of a grander spectacle of yester-year!

Walk up the path to the right of the bridge and then left over the canal. Immediately on the other side take the path leading down to the canal towpath. The canal and path meander through open countryside but keep your eyes open for wildfowl and hedgerow birds. During my walk along here I was fortunate to see a heron who let me reach within ten yards and then flew a little further down the canal. In just over half a mile leave the towpath by the path to the side of the bridge. The Navigation pub provides liquid refreshment and a garden by the canal (3).

Cross over the bridge and down to the towpath on the opposite side of the canal. Continue along the path and under a brick bridge in about three quarters of a mile, until an iron girder bridge is reached in a further half mile (4). A few yards before this bridge turn right up the path and left across the bridge and onto a farm track. Traffic can be seen along the main road and this is soon reached.

Cross the main road (5) and follow along the minor road marked Yardley Gobion and Pottersbury. Do not turn right for the village but continue for about three hundred yards until you find a sign on the right, partly hidden in the hedge and marked Public Footpath to Yardley Gobion to the right and Old Stratford to the left (6).

Cross over the stile situated in the hedge on the left side of the road and continue along the path with the hedge immediately on your right.

This leads through attractive open countryside and Furtho Church in the distance. The footpath is reasonably well marked and goes through two fields until the point where there are about six trees forming a small copse. Bear slightly right and keep the hedge and the trees on your left. There is also a stream with rabbits and voles scurrying around diving in and out of the holes in the bank.

After about a hundred yards the stream, path and hedge turn sharp right (7). Furtho Church is easily spotted through the trees. Soon a plank over a small stream leads into a field - full of new born lambs when I was there. A delightful spring sight which ended with the equally idyllic setting of Furtho pond, church and dovecote. This is reached at the end of the field by crossing over a bridge and stile and walking to the right of the pond.

At this point the walk joins the Grafton Way - look for the signs, which mark the remainder of the walk. Continue towards the church, although you may wish to take a closer look at the dovecote. Cross over the stile by the church and then walk diagonally across the field towards a stile (8) in the hedge. Over the stile and then sharp left along the tarmac farm road and up towards the main road.

The Grafton Way is marked at the junction of the main road. Cross over the A508 and continue along the minor road towards Cosgrove. In about two hundred yards the road branches to the left and is marked Castlethorpe and Hanslope. The Grafton Way continues over a stile (9) and into a field immediately to the right. Keep the hedge on your right.

After a few minutes you will find a stile in the hedge in the corner of a field. Cross over this and an a second which leads you around the edge of Rectory Farm. Good sign posts mark the Grafton Way.

The path leads through a gate and into a field. Do not take the footpath to the right but continue straight ahead along the Grafton Way.

Walk through two fields and finally past houses on the edge of Cosgrove village. A stile takes you into a lane and down to the main road. Turn right and up towards the church. Cross the road and the Grafton Way continues through the churchyard. Again well signposted.

Leave the churchyard footpath and walk down towards the Barley Mow and the end of your walk.

Northampton: River Nene and Rush Mills

SUMMARY: This walk is particularly beautiful alongside the River Nene. Take binoculars as the area is rich in bird life. On each occasion that I have walked this route there has been a flock of Canada Geese on the far bank of the river but look for other birds too.

ATTRACTIONS: Northampton dates back to at least the eighth century. Early archaeological excavations close to St Peter's Church suggest that there may have been an early Saxon settlement nearby, although the first registered record of Hamtune's existence was in 914.

St Peter's Church has many Norman features including the tower and arches. The decorative arcading on the nave arches and the pier carvings is fabulous.

In the eleventh century Simon de Senlis fortified the town with walls and built a castle. Other buildings he was responsible for included the famous round church of The Holy Sepulchre. Although neither the castle or town walls remain the Church of the Holy Sepulchre is one of four round churches left in England and is worth visiting.

Further along the Bedford Road, (the start of your walk), and towards the town is Becket's Well. It was during the twelfth century that Becket suffered continual injustice from King Henry II and much of his time was spent in Northampton and he became a local hero. Tradition says that when Thomas Becket was fleeing from Northampton Castle he stopped at the well to drink from a spring. Later Becket was martyred in Canterbury Cathedral, where his shrine is today.

Rush Mills was originally used for corn grinding and dates back at least to the thirteenth century. Like all mills, in its heyday it was a valuable source of power but with the development of railways and roads during the nineteenth and twentieth centuries it became redundant and in 1985 was demolished. The mill site is just opposite The Britannia Inn.

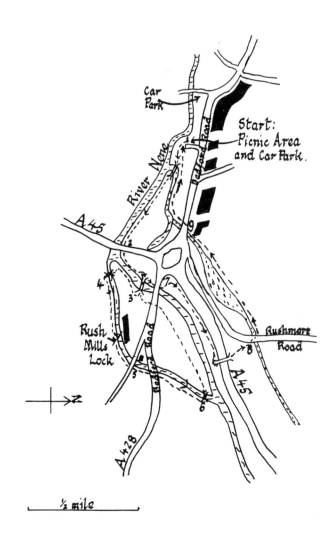

Car
Park

Start:
Picnic Area
and Car Park.

River Nene

Bedford Road

A 45

Rush
Mills
Lock

Bedford Road

A 45

Rushmere
Road

A 428

N

½ mile

46

START: Begin your walk at the picnic area and car park situated alongside the Bedford Road. This is within easy access of the town centre.

ROUTE: From the Bedford Road Picnic Area (1) walk towards the bridge over a backwater of the Nene. Cross the bridge and turn immediately left to follow the Nene Way. The first half of the walk follows the well signposted Nene Way. Look for the flock of Canada Geese. Continue alongside the river until reaching the main A45 and bridge (2).

Walk under the bridge and continue along the river making for the small bridge next to the main sluice gates. Cross this bridge and turn immediately right onto a tarmac footpath (3).

Continue along the path until reaching another small footbridge. Cross this and then immediately turn left to follow the Nene Way along the bank of the river (4).

The lock at Rush Mills soon appears and the new Waterside Office development. This is a small very attractive office park. Cross over the stile and under the A428 Bedford Road. The Britannia Inn with its stocks is across the river on the left (5).

The walk continues along a gravel footpath and obviously newly landscaped to fit in with the office development shortly to be started. Pass Abington Lock and stile making for the bridge over the river (6).

Do not follow the Nene Way ahead but turn left through a gate, over a bridge and along the ridge and flood route towards Northampton. The new stone path way with the Holiday Inn on your left leads you to the main Bedford Road. The main dual carriageway road is to your right.

Cross over the Bedford Road and through a small car park making for the sluice gate and Point 3. Cross the bridge and turn right (do not turn left - this takes you to your starting point). Follow the tarmac path under the Bedford Road and around to the left (7).

The river is now on your right. In about 500 yards the path leads to a bridge across the main road. Cross the bridge and down to Rushmere Road (8). Cross over the road and your walk continues along the path by the side of the flood channel and lake. This is signposted to Northampton and the Town Centre.

In about half a mile the path reaches the Bedford Road roundabout with a private entrance to St Andrew's Hospital on your immediate right (9). Cross the main road and walk alongside the river to your starting point.

WALK 13   5.5 miles

Northampton: Becket's Park - Carlsberg Brewery - River Nene -
Upton Mill - Grand Union Canal - Becket's Park

SUMMARY: The walk follows the Nene Way footpath through the southern end of Northampton and opens out into countryside beside the River Nene. The walk follows the river to the old Upton Mill and then returns alongside the Grand Union Canal with Briar Hill Estate on the right. Although the early part of the walk is through the town the river is quite beautiful and the complete walk one not to be missed.

ATTRACTIONS: Becket's Park, named after Thomas a Becket, who spent much of his time in Northampton and was Archbishop of Canterbury between 1162 and 1170, was for many generations known as Cow Meadow, a place for grazing cattle.

Calvesholme Lake is on a picturesque island situated in a conservation area and is specifically a bird sanctuary. This area looks over to the Avon Cosmetic factory which was built in 1959 and stands on the site of the old mill called Nunn Mills. The mill was demolished in 1970 and the site further developed. There are two large mill stones which can be seen by turning left at point 1 and walking across the bridge. Situated on the right, the mill stones and commemorative plaque mark the mill site which probably stood there for 800 years. The name Nunn Mills is derived from the nunnery at Delapre.

It was also in this area that the Battle of Northampton was fought on 10 July 1460. This battle was one of the early battles in the Wars of the Roses and was fought close to the River Nene and the mill. Henry VI was defeated, taken to London and eventually deposed by Edward IV, son of Richard, Duke of York. The early part of the walk through to the London Road (A508) looks out over the river and towards the battlefield - sadly now built over with factories.

The Express Lift Tower has become a land mark in Northampton since

49

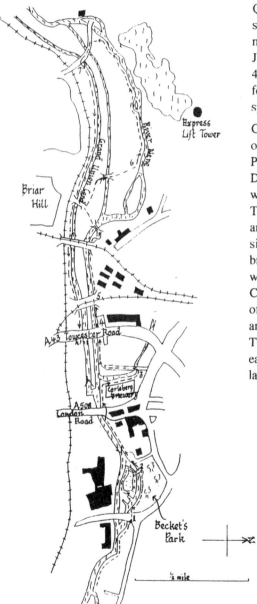

it was opened by the Queen in 1982. It stands where the medieval Abbey of St James once stood. The 418 foot tower is used for the testing of high speed lifts.

Carlsberg Brewery was opened in 1974 by Princess Benedikte of Denmark. The design won the Financial Times award in 1975 and is situated on the site of a previous brewery. Northampton was chosen for the Carlsberg site because of its central position and good routeways. Thus allowing for the easy distribution of its lager.

50

START: Begin your walk from the car park and picnic area as in Walk 12. This park is clearly marked and is situated alongside the Bedford Road.

ROUTE: Walk along the river towards the town and the bridge which leads to the Avon factory and Nunn Mills Road (1). Walk over the road and continue alongside the river and through Becket's Park. Cross over the footbridge (2) and follow the right hand footpath around the island with Calvesholme Lake in the centre. Returning to point 2, turn left to continue your walk through the park.

The walk continues around the back of the Cattle Market and towards South Bridge on the main London Road. Cross over the road and return back to the riverside walk. Here the smell of Carlsberg Brewery, built in the early seventies, fills the air. The walk traverses the brewery boundary and follows a small tributary of the river.

Where the path reaches the Carlsberg entrance (3) redouble your walk along the other side of the tributary until you rejoin the main river. Turn right onto a stone path which takes you around the back of the Gas works and then under the Towcester Road. To the right is a new shopping area with car parks (4).

If you want a shorter walk of about three miles then begin at this point.

Continue along the river and under the main railway bridge (5). A second railway bridge soon appears. Under this and turn left over the river at the next bridge. The walk continues along a tarmac path across open land and towards Briar Hill Estate. Turn right at the next footbridge, without crossing the bridge and make back towards the river, another bridge and the Express Lift Tower.

Cross the bridge and over the stile walking immediately ahead towards the tower and river. As you rejoin the main river there is the remains of a weir. Turn left (6) and continue along the river bank. After about half a mile bear left and down to a farm track. Turn left and follow the track towards the estate. Over the first bridge and on towards the canal (7).

Turn left after crossing the second bridge and go down to the canal towpath. Walk along the towpath with Briar Hill estate on your right. The towpath soon becomes adjacent to the disused railway line.

51

Continue along the towpath under two railway bridges and soon after the second one walk under the Towcester Road and immediately double back right up the bank and onto the road.

If you have taken the shorter route then your walk finishes here at Point 4.

For those walkers who started from the Bedford Road picnic spot then rejoin the first part of the walk across the Towcester Road.

Return past the brewery, the cattle market and Becket's Park to the car park.

Wellingborough railway viaduct - Walk 14

WALK 14   5 miles

Irchester Country Park - Irchester Village - River Nene -
Wellingborough Embankment - Irchester Country Park

SUMMARY: A gentle walk beginning in one of Northamptonshire's beautiful country parks. This largely woodland park offers a variety of flora and fauna. The walk continues through the outskirts of Irchester and along the Nene Valley.

ATTRACTIONS: The country park was opened in 1971 on land which had previously been worked for ironstone and there are many walks around the area. Paths are interspersed between springs and marshy land with shrubs and wild flowers covering the scars left by quarrying. The park is a good base to start and finish your walk.

Irchester village dates back to the Iron Age and has also yielded evidence from the Romano-British period. The name Irchester comes from the Anglo Saxon Iren Ceastre meaning iron fortress or town. St Katherine's Church stands on a site occupied by buildings of worship since the thirteenth century. The church is an attractive building of limestone and ironstone, materials which would have been easily found in the area. It is interesting to see the weather vane which includes the catherine wheel in its design. It is thought that Saint Katherine the saint whom the church is consecrated after might have been tortured to death on a catherine wheel!

Wellingborough has an interesting church next to the Market Place. All Hallows, built largely during the thirteenth and fourteenth centuries, has a Norman south door, a spire 165 feet in height and an interesting window commemorating a victim of the Civil War. Nearby is the old sixteenth century grammar school and an old fifteenth century tithe barn.

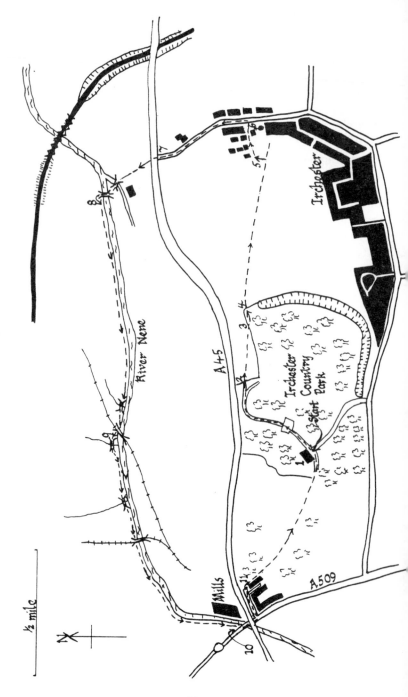

River Nene

Irchester

A 45

Irchester Country Park

Start

Mills

A.509

½ mile

N

54

START: Irchester Country Park is situated off the A509 approximately one and a half miles from Wellingborough. There is ample car park space.

ROUTE: Begin your walk from the Visitor's Information Centre (1) by turning right in a north easterly direction as you face the centre. Walk through the small car park and onto one of the park tracks. The first half of the walk follows the Nene Way footpath. Continue along the track until you reach the point where the track turns to the right and is only a few yards from the Wellingborough bypass (A45).

In about sixty yards look for the sign pointing left which briefly takes you back into the woods and off the main track. In a few yards the path continues over a stile and out across open fields (2). At this point the path is not clearly marked but walk diagonally across to the right making for a spot not quite in the corner of the wood (3). A stile in the hedge is quite clearly marked and also has the Nene Way sign.

Cross over the stile, keep left and after a few yards rejoin the country park track. Again after a few yards the track turns right but the walk bears left and up a flight of steps to a stile and open fields (4). Irchester church spire can be clearly seen in the distance. The walk continues ahead through the field along a path.

Continue across the field with superb views of the Nene Valley to the left and the village of Irchester immediately ahead. Do not turn left down an obvious track in the middle of the field but continue until meeting an old wall. Turn left here and follow the edge of the field with the hedge immediately on your right. A few yards along the hedge there is a marked stile (5). Cross over the stile and across the field making for the church.

The path follows the edge of the churchyard, then over another stile and into the churchyard. In a few yards the path leads into a tarmac lane and down between houses with Barringers Gardens and Court on the left.

At the main road turn left to follow the Nene Way footpath (6). Continue along this road out of Irchester. In about half a mile cross the main A45, take care - its a busy road (7). The steps lead down towards the River Nene. Go through the gate and walk straight across the field marked, Public Footpath to Wellingborough.

At this spot there are good views of the railway viaduct across the river.

Cross the small tributary of the River Nene by the farm house on the left. Continue towards and across the second footbridge and then turn left and walk along the banks of the river (8). The Nene Way footpath turns right at this point. I was lucky to see a swan on her nest, a heron and a jay all around this area.

There are no footpath signs now until Wellingborough embankment is reached. Follow the river until crossing over a bridge under which a small stream feeds the main river. In a dry summer the stream may be dried up! Over a stile and pass under the old railway bridge to a footbridge the other side (9).

A footpath to Wellingborough goes off to the right here. Continue to walk alongside the river bank and past a guillotine lock. This is a private fishing area for the Wellingborough and District Nene Angling Club.

A short walk over several small and often dried up streams eventually leads you over a stile and into a fenced area prior to Wellingborough embankment. Pass under the old railway bridge and along the embankment adjacent to which is a minor road, before meeting the main A509 (10).

Immediately before this road turn sharp right and walk up the side of the bridge onto the road. There is a brown post at this point and on the reverse side is marked the direction of the Nene Way footpath. On the bridge turn left, there is a sign post marking the Nene Way, which in a few yards takes you under the busy A45 Wellingborough bypass.

The entrance to Whitworth Mill and factory is on the left. In a few yards turn left into Daniels Road passing the War Memorial and also marked the Nene Way. This road is adjacent to the A45. At the end of the road our walk turns right into Irchester Country Park (11).

The cinder footpath follows the Nene Way signs back to the centre of the park passing Irchester Narrow Gauge Railway Museum which is open on certain days of the year.

WALK 15   4 miles

Rothersthorpe - **Grand Union Canal** - **Gayton Marina** -

Rothersthorpe

(Additional walk to Blisworth and the Tunnel)

SUMMARY: This is a gentle walk along the canals and countryside around Rothersthorpe. The walk passes through Gayton Marina and junction and in the summer is extremely busy with holiday makers.

ATTRACTIONS: Rothersthorpe village is situated on the Banbury Lane road which is thought to have been part of the prehistoric "Jurassic Way", a ridgeway from south-west to north-east Britain. At the centre of the village is the "The Berry" or "Bury" the site of an Iron Age settlement. It was also in this area, that possibly in AD 918 the Saxon army of Edward the Elder defeated the Danish forces who were occupying Northampton. The church of St Peter and St Paul has possibly seventh century origins - the base of a preaching cross of this age has been found and a Norman font gives further early historical evidence.

Blisworth, if you take the extended walk, in its heyday was a busy section of the Grand Union Canal with its many wharfs handling a variety of cargo - bricks, lime, coal, etc. Today the canalside mill is used by a boat firm as a boatyard with all the usual facilities. The canal disappears into the darkness of Blisworth tunnel which is still the longest tunnel, 3075 yards long, in use on the Waterways system. The entrance is certainly worth a visit. Blisworth church has the original rood screen stairs, and large dark brown tablets either side of the altar on which are written the Ten Commandments. There is also an altar tomb in the south aisle to Roger and Elizabeth Wake. Roger Wake was sheriff of the county in 1483.

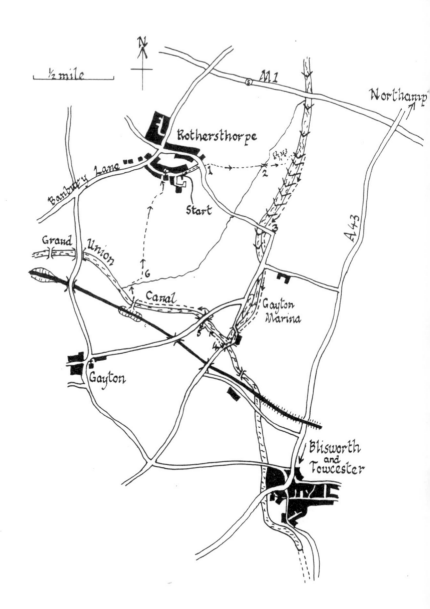

½ mile

N

M1

Northamp

Rothersthorpe

Banbury Lane

1

P.W.

2

Start

3

Grand Union

A43

Canal

6

Gayton Marina

5

Gayton

Blisworth
and
Towcester

START: The walk starts in Rothersthorpe village which is south of Northampton and to the west of the main A43. There is ample car parking space in this quiet village. Begin your walk by the church in Church Street.

ROUTE: Walk down Church Street and past "The Manor" on the right. At the end of the road there is a footpath marked, Public Footpath to Lady Bridge, which leads into the field on the opposite side of the road (1). Follow this path across the field.

At the first hedge turn right keeping the hedge on your left. The path is well worn. Continue by the side of the hedge until the path arrives at a small flat concrete bridge over a stream (2). Cross over the stream and continue to follow the path to the left and adjacent to the hedge.

There is a slight incline to the canal with a wood on the left. The canal towpath is on the far side so cross over the canal using one of the lock gates.

Turn right along the towpath passing numerous lock gates of many shapes and varieties. This section of the canal which links the main Grand Union to the River Nene and Northampton has thirteen lock gates and three quaint lift bridges and is known as the Rothersthorpe Flight.

Pass under the Rothersthorpe to Milton Malsor road (3) and the lock keepers cottage and then under the road again! The canal is very busy here as the walk continues past mobile homes, narrowboat dwellers and through Gayton Marina.

Leave the towpath after Bridge 2 built in 1912 and return to the towpath after passing Gayton Maintenance Yard and The Old Toll House. You are now at Gayton Junction on the Grand Union Canal (4). Braunston 16.5 miles, Northampton 4.75 miles, Brentford 77 miles, Birmingham and London are all marked.

Continue along the towpath signposted to Birmingham. At the first minor road the towpath crosses to the other side of the canal. This is achieved via a unique double bridge known as Turnover Bridge and does not require the walker to use the main road (5).

In about half a mile a steel girder bridge is reached. Turn right away from the canal and into the field. The path signposts are not well marked although the farmer has left good walking space between the hedge and the crops. Keep the hedge on your right until reaching a small wooden bridge in the corner of the field.

Cross over the stream. Turn immediately right and continue keeping the hedge on your right. At the junction of the next field pass through and turn immediately left keeping the hedge on your left (6). At the end of the field you can see the saddleback tower of Rothersthorpe church - your finishing point.

Continue by crossing the track keeping the hedge on your left. At the end of the field cross over the stile and walk across the field to another stile and footpath sign pointing in the direction from which you have just come.

This leads out into a beautiful cul-de-sac adjacent to the church and the completion of your walk.

This walk can be extended by a further four miles by walking towards Blisworth at Gayton Junction and then returning via the road or canal to the Junction.

Grey heron

WALK 16   5 miles

Kings Sutton - River Cherwell - Oxford Canal -

Kings Sutton

SUMMARY: An easy walk through some beautiful countryside and following the course between the River Cherwell and the Oxford Canal.

ATTRACTIONS: Kings Sutton is a peaceful and quaint old village with many old houses dating from the sixteenth and seventeenth centuries. If you have time to take the path through Astrop Park you will pass the site of St Rumbold's Well - the waters of which were recommended during the seventeenth century to help solve stomach disorders! The church of St Peter and St Paul is worth a visit. The outstanding feature is the spire which has a height of 198 feet and was built during the first half of the fifteenth century. The original church was probably of Saxon origin - the font is certainly Saxon and is associated with the Baptism of St Rumbold. The chancel stands on Norman foundations and the remainder of the church has been added to since then. The altar is dedicated to St Thomas of Canterbury whom it is said may have prayed on his way to Northampton Castle in October 1164.

King's Sutton Church

Both the church and the village are worth exploring.

61

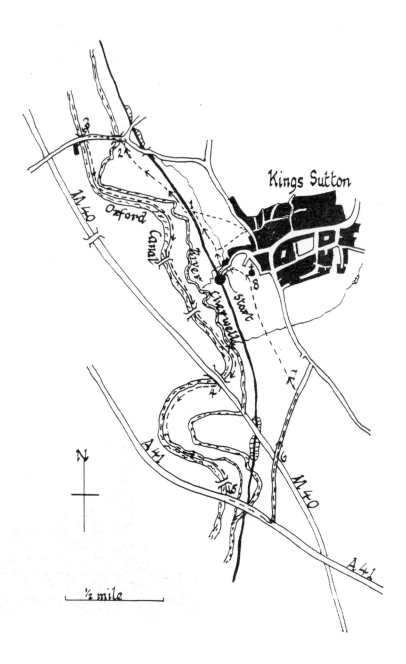

Kings Sutton

Oxford Canal

River Cherwell

Start

N

½ mile

A41

M40

START: Kings Sutton is south west of Brackley and a few miles from Banbury. It is situated on the Northamptonshire and Oxfordshire border just off the A41. There are ample car parking facilities at Kings Sutton station.

ROUTE: Start from the station car park by taking the only road back into the village. After a few yards look for the sign on the left "Public Footpath To Twyford Bridge". The sign and path are between the houses and next to Willow Cottage (No 50).

Follow the path over a stream and stile into a field. The path is well trodden and parallel to the railway line which is about fifty yards to the left.

Continue through two small fields and over two stiles, the second one bearing slightly to the left and over a small bridge and stile towards the railway line. The path fades out but walk alongside the railway line looking for the stile which leads over the railway line (1).

There is a warning by the stile to: STOP, LOOK, LISTEN, BEWARE OF TRAINS!

Cross the railway line. The path over to the right and the road and bridge is not well marked. Take one of three routes. Keep to the right and close to the railway line, follow the river bank around, or continue through the field if the path is marked. Any of these routes will lead to the bridge over the River Cherwell (2).

Cross over the bridge into Oxfordshire and continue along the road to the canal bridge (3). Turn right down to the towpath, back under the bridge and continue alongside the Oxford Canal. This is a beautiful and picturesque part of the canal. You will pass Kings Sutton Lock and several wooden bridges which are raised and lowered to enable farmers to cross the canal to farm their land.

Walk under the new M40 (4).

At Nell Bridge Lock walk up the path to the main A41 (5).

Continue left along the road, cross over the River Cherwell and back into Northamptonshire. Turn left along the minor road and over the main M40 (6).

Soon after the M40 look for the footpath sign which leads over a stile and into a superbly marked footpath (7). Thank you to the local farmer for leaving the path through the middle of his field. The walk continues by heading straight for the church.

Cross several stiles, a wooden bridge and stream, all well marked, until reaching the field adjacent to the church (8). Keeping the church on your right walk through the middle of the field until reaching a sign "Public Footpath". Cross over the stile and walk down through the field to the station and your starting point.

WALK 17   2.5 miles

Harlestone - Lower Harlestone - Upper Harlestone - Harlestone

SUMMARY: Although not a true waterside walk, this is a picturesque part of Northamptonshire where there are constant views of Harlestone Lake. Harlestone is a typical Northamptonshire village, full of character with old thatched cottages built of local stone. This is a short walk full of charm and interest and is ideal for a summer evening or weekend afternoon with lots of space for children to run and explore.

ATTRACTIONS: Harlestone village has been greatly influenced by the Spencer's of Althorp who purchased the Harlestone Estate from the Andrew's family early in the nineteenth century. The Spencer's, the Princess of Wales' family, helped the social and economic development of the village but now fewer local people depend upon agriculture and the estate for their livelihood.

In 1745 Bonnie Prince Charlie heard that the Northamptonians were grouped at Harlestone and so halted his army and returned to Scotland being defeated at the Battle of Culloden.

The ancient circular dovecote, only two hundred yards further down the road from point 9, is worth visiting. It is probably fourteenth century and at one time had nests for over four hundred birds.

Harlestone Dovecote

65

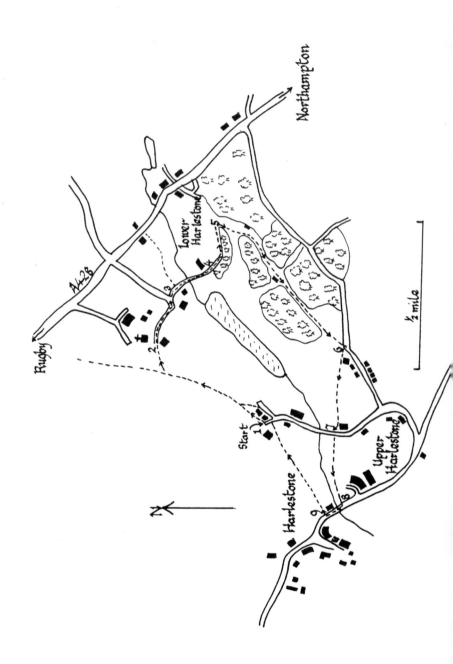

START: Harlestone village lies three and a half miles north-west of Northampton and just off the A428 road to Rugby. Park the car by the village green, next to the village hall.

ROUTE: Take the footpath (1) to the right of the village hall, which is sign posted and leads behind the back of the cottages and post office. Do not follow the signs to the playing fields. After a few yards this tarmac path is joined by another coming from the other end of the cottages. After the first gate the footpath widens slightly and crosses the farm track.

Follow the path down towards the right side of the church wall (2). At the bottom is the main church yard entrance gate and the path widens and turns to the right.

Continue down the path. The imposing building of Harlestone House is on the left behind the wall. In about a hundred yards several quaint thatched cottages appear clustered together by Harlestone School. The left road leads to the main road. Continue your walk by crossing the road making for the farm track with Autumn Cottage on your right.

Continue along this track (3) - but be prepared, it is invariably muddy. Do not take the footpath left into the field. Continue past Lake Cottage, over the stream and up towards the farm on your left. On your right there is what appears to be a road side well. One of several to be found on this walk and around Harlestone.

Go through the gate (4). The farm track follows the edge of the wood and deviates around to the left whilst opening out into a field.

At the corner of the wood there are two footpath signs and another wood clearly defined immediately in front of you. Turn right (5) and walk between the two woods. After about seventy yards cross over the farm track - notice the cottage on the far left and the clearing on the right which leads through to the lake.

Continue walking alongside the wood making for the gate by the cottages ahead. Walk through the gate and along the track to a very minor road.

Cross over the road and continue your walk between the two woods. After two hundred and fifty yards the woods stop and the path takes you across an open field to the road.

Go through the gate and almost immediately to the right, and before the houses, there is a stile in the wall (6). Go over the stile and into the field keeping the garden fences on your left. At the corner of the fencing, walk diagonally to the left and across the field, making for a stile.

Go over the stile and walk across the field towards the gate in the corner. This opens out into a drive of a private house and onto the road (7). Walk straight across the road, through the gate and onto a tarmac footpath. The path takes you through another gate and alongside a pretty stream with birds and wildlife in abundance, and this despite the houses of Upper Harlestone on the bank to the left.

The next gate opens out onto the road (8). Turn right and in about fifty yards and immediately after the thatched cottage, turn right through the gate (9) and into the field. The tarmac path leads through another gate and returns you to the village hall and your starting point.

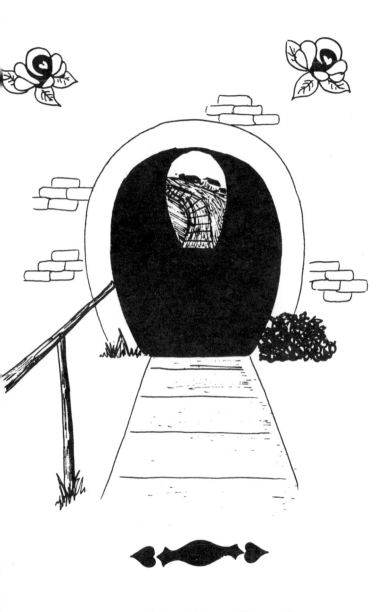

Canal tunnel, Cosgrove - Walks 10 & 11

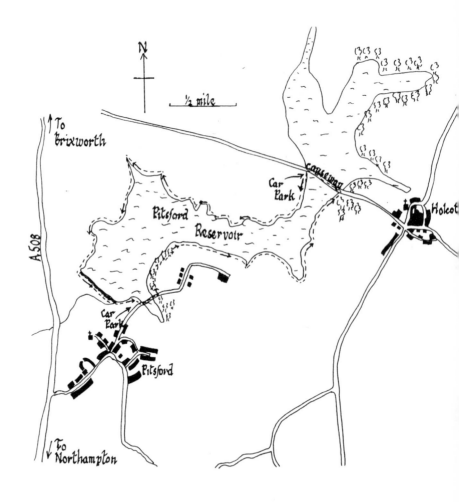

N

½ mile

To
Brixworth

Pitsford
Reservoir

Causeway

Car
Park

Car
Park

A508

Pitsford

Hoket

To
Northampton

RESERVOIRS AND LAKES

WALK 18   6.5 miles

Pitsford Reservoir

SUMMARY: These next three reservoirs and lakes all give the walker the opportunity for an easy circular walk with an abundance of wildlife to see and admire. The three walks are of varying length and offer a variety of picnic spots and if required can be extended to include the local villages.

Pitsford Reservoir is about five miles north of Northampton and is situated between the A508 Northampton to Market Harborough road and the A43 Northampton to Kettering road.

There are two main areas to begin your walk. Either the car park just outside Pitsford village or the car park by the causeway on the Holcot to Brixworth road. Both are suitable points to begin and the walk can be achieved in either direction.

The walk follows closely the banks of the reservoir. Enjoy the flora, fauna and the waterbirds. The reservoir is the winter home for about a thousand wildfowl. Tufted ducks, pochard and shovelars are all found around the waters.

Pitsford village church is the oldest building in the village. It has a thirteenth century tower and a Norman doorway but much of the remaining building was restored during the nineteenth century. There is also what is thought to be a longbarrow on the road leading out towards the main A508. Known as Longman's Hill Round Barrow it is thought to be of Saxon or even of the Bronze Age - what is certain, it is an important burial mound, as was proven when in the early nineteenth century skeletons were found when the barrow was cut during road widening.

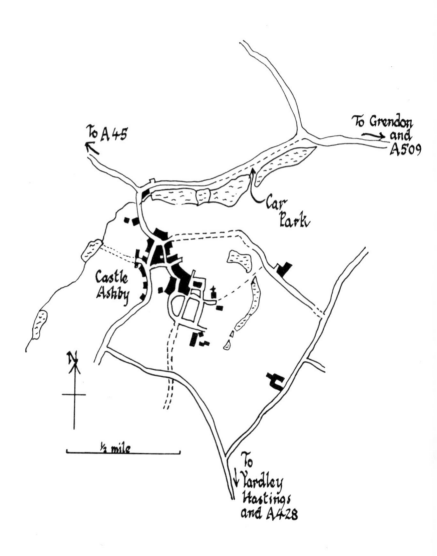

To A45

To Grendon
and
A509

Car
Park

Castle
Ashby

N

½ mile

To
Yardley
Hastings
and A428

Castle Ashby Lakes

Castle Ashby Lakes are situated south of the main A45 Northampton to Wellingborough road and in the estate belonging to the Earl of Northampton. Although a much shorter walk than the other two it is nevertheless well worth spending an afternoon walking around the lakes and taking a detour into Castle Ashby and walking around the estate.

Park either by the lakes or in the village.

Castle Ashby House stands in most luxurious surroundings and has a splendid avenue of trees leading through from Yardley Hastings. The grounds, parklands and lakes are open daily, the house only occasionally. The church built during the thirteenth century was also part of several buildings including a chantry and castle. Sir William Compton bought the estate in 1512 and in 1612 the then Lord Compton was made Earl of Northampton and it continues to be the Earl's seat today. In the churchyard are some remarkable memorials to the Compton family.

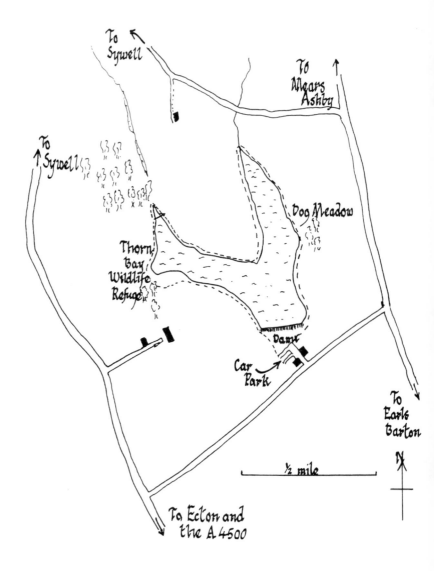

To Sywell

To Mears Ashby

To Sywell

Dog Meadow

Thorn Bay Wildlife Refuge

Dam

Car Park

To Earls Barton

To Ecton and the A 4500

½ mile

N

74

WALK 19   0.75 miles

Castle Ashby Lakes

Castle Ashby Lakes are situated south of the main A45 Northampton to Wellingborough road and in the estate belonging to the Earl of Northampton. Although a much shorter walk than the other two it is nevertheless well worth spending an afternoon walking around the lakes and taking a detour into Castle Ashby and walking around the estate.

Park either by the lakes or in the village.

Castle Ashby House stands in most luxurious surroundings and has a splendid avenue of trees leading through from Yardley Hastings. The grounds, parklands and lakes are open daily, the house only occasionally. The church built during the thirteenth century was also part of several buildings including a chantry and castle. Sir William Compton bought the estate in 1512 and in 1612 the then Lord Compton was made Earl of Northampton and it continues to be the Earl's seat today. In the churchyard are some remarkable memorials to the Compton family.

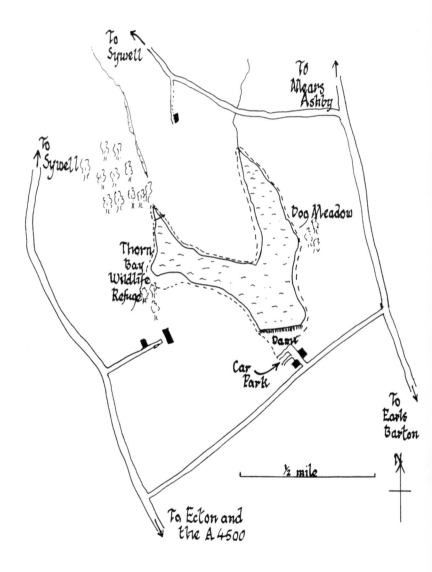

To Sywell

To Mears Ashby

To Sywell

Dog Meadow

Thorn Bay Wildlife Refuge

Dam

Car Park

To Earls Barton

½ mile

N

To Ecton and the A 4500

74

WALK 20   2.5 miles

Sywell Reservoir

Sywell Reservoir is situated within Sywell Country Park and between the main A43 Northampton to Kettering and the A4500 Northampton to Wellingborough roads. Although the reservoir was opened in 1906 it only became a country park in 1985 when no longer needed to provide water for the local towns.

The area around the entrance and the car park is a mixture of open meadow, woodland and picnic spots. The RSPB in conjunction with the country park have developed much of this area and encouraged a variety of bird life to live within the habitat. Fishing is limited to permit members and tench, pike, perch and roach are common to the reservoir.

The walk around the reservoir will take you through reed beds. marshland, open pasture and woodland. In this wildlife refuge you will find the homes of many water birds.